Tapping Into
YOUR PERSONAL PRESENCE

BRIAN ROSCOE

TAPPING INTO YOUR PERSONAL PRESENCE
COPYRIGHT © 2021 BY BRIAN ROSCOE

All rights reserved. No part of this publication may be reproduced, distributed, or transmitted in any form or by any means, including photocopying, recording, or other electronic or mechanical methods, without the prior written permission of the author, except in the case of brief quotations embodied in critical reviews and certain other noncommercial uses permitted by copyright law.

The content of this book is for general informational purposes only. It is not meant to be used, nor should it be used, to diagnose or treat any medical condition or to replace the services of your physician or other healthcare provider. The advice and strategies contained in the book may not be suitable for all readers.

Neither the author, publisher, nor any of their employees or representatives guarantees the accuracy of information in this book or its usefulness to a particular reader, nor are they responsible for any damage or negative consequence that may result from any treatment, action taken, or inaction by any person reading or following the information in this book.

For permission requests or to contact the author, visit:
brianroscoeauthor.com

ISBN-13: 978-1-957348-08-7

PRINTED IN THE UNITED STATES OF AMERICA

Tapping Into YOUR PERSONAL PRESENCE

> *"I don't have to chase extraordinary moments to find happiness—it's right in front of me if I'm paying attention and practicing gratitude."*
> -Brené Brown

For me, in the mindfulness of presence, I become aware of that fine thread of energy that emanates through me and connects with everything else that exists. It doesn't matter whether I can see it, or even whether I know of its existence. All that matters is that it is. This quality of presence to life, a knowingness, is an understanding that flows through me, and it lets me know that very part of me, the tiniest speck of my essence, is connected to and sharing some quality of life with every other part of everything that is.

This full presence fills every part of me. It smells like fresh rain, or the breeze of a spring morning. It feels like standing in the power of the sun, eyes closed, caught up in absorption. It's somehow similar to the innocence of a young child, pure in its participation, alive with its gift. I feel it electrically through my body, I sense it in the golden line of energy flowing through each chakra. It is life showered down from the heavens above, moving up and through me from the earth below. This is where my spirit sings, where my body becomes aware of its infinite form, presence to my world keeps my mind open to gratitude and every sense stimulated with the electricity of life.

Can you remember or be open to moments of presence for yourself?

What did that feel like, smell like, how does it look to you, and what did you feel?

Tapping Into YOUR PERSONAL PRESENCE

Your essence existed before you. It was an energy, a flow, an expanding flower of light, present at your conception, infusing you with a cosmic perfume created only for you. Anything that you are after that is not less than your essence simply contributes to it—your knowing, your feelings, your thoughts. Prior to any of these, your essence is what you were, and your essence is what you will return to. Knowing, remembering essence, is our goal, just as remembering love is. This is our journey. It's how we find and embrace every form of the love that we are.

ON POWER STATEMENTS

Sometimes our moments of awareness and insight can feel like they've taken on a "fad" quality. The warrior in you has a profound breakthrough in the way you see the world, and, suddenly, everyone's commenting on *your* new understanding—we discover that we are not alone in our revelations. This is when we begin to explore our new understanding through other people's perspectives, conjoining those findings with our own.

This human journey, *our journey*, has been written about for years, probably millennia, and there's no question that you're not the first

Tapping Into YOUR PERSONAL PRESENCE

to have any particular thought, no matter how profound, and you won't be the last. So, as you step into your new understandings of how your world works, you'll notice that everyone is talking about or writing on your insight (start looking to buy a red car and suddenly you see red cars everywhere!).

As you look further, you see that one very special, particular quote really touches you, it infects your being, and you know you've found that sparkling and perfect phrase, sentence, or word that touches your heart and invigorates your spirit. Well... there it is! There's your *Power Statement*—the phrase that brings forward the juice of life. It doesn't matter where or how it came to you. It's there! It gets crowned forever as one of your phrases of strength, forever, or at least until the next generation of wisdom pokes its head up!

JOURNEY PROMPT

How's that Power Statement list coming? Stay open to all the new stuff, all the funny moments, all the happenstance ways the universe feeds the list! There's your homework: feed your list!

The perception of how we experience our environment comes down to how we're choosing to hold our life—not so much in how we believe life is holding us.

Tapping Into YOUR PERSONAL PRESENCE

JOURNEY PROMPT

In my early twenties, I remember greeting a friend in his sixties with the question, "Hey, Jack, how's life treating you?" His answer stayed with me all my life. It was simple, a bit cliché, but, as a young guy, it hit me hard in that moment. He said, "It's great! You know, Brian, I find it's not so much how life is treating me, but how I'm treating life." And we both smiled and walked on into our day.

How we perceive our personal life experience is largely dependent on choice. Do we choose to see life as kind or aggressive, would we approach it with understanding or as intolerable? Because our experience here is not so much based in how we believe life is treating us, but on how we're treating life.

"True intelligence operates silently. Stillness is where creativity and solutions to problems are found."
-Eckhart Tolle

We get to choose who we are, we get choose what we are.

When we mindfully step back and look at the seemingly infinite variety of experiences that are presented to us daily, almost by the second, our opportunities for life seem massive. Couple that with the ability to choose how we want to interact with any experience or event. Our responses to events can range from understanding to angry, compassionate to resentful, from jealous to joyful, and fearful to loving. There is an infinite potential surrounding our human experience. We can choose and independently alter how we see our life, and we can see any event through a countless number of lenses, which only we can select.

With all this potential life experience placed in our hands, why would we choose a lens that focuses on anything less than love? Why would we choose to direct our attention elsewhere? Focus on what has meaning, because if you miss love, you miss life.

**We get to choose who we are,
we get choose what we are.**

JOURNEY PROMPT

Do a little thought experiment with yourself:

Take a benign situation, something that you really don't have any attachment to, like the color of your car, drinking a glass of water, or putting your socks on, and imagine attaching to different emotions around that particular circumstance. For example, you're putting your socks on and you attach one at a time to these emotions: grateful, resentful, fearful, loving, angry, joyful. It's your choice. And it directly impacts the quality of the experience of that particular event. This is true more times than you would care to admit, in more events than you can even begin to make up. We've been trained to react in particular ways to particular situations, and it's part of the journey of the warrior to respond in ways that bring strength and honor to this life, no matter what life presents.

Tapping Into YOUR PERSONAL PRESENCE

We make ourselves so mindlessly busy, denying our mortality and being so scared of death, that we forget to live, we forget to be in each breath, to recognize each moment of living presented to us right now. We get so caught up in avoiding or nurturing our fear of death that we forget death is only a change in our spark of life, and our real goal is to fully live in and embrace our spark, no matter what form it comes to us in.

"So, live your life that the fear of death can never enter your heart. Trouble no one about their religion; respect others in their view, and demand that they respect yours. Love your life, perfect your life, beautify all things in your life. Seek to make your life long and its purpose in the service of your people. Prepare a noble death song for the day when you go over the great divide. Always give a word or a sign of salute when meeting or passing a friend, even a stranger, when in a lonely place. Show respect to all people

and bow to none. When you arise in the morning, give thanks for the food and for the joy of living. If you see no reason for giving thanks, the fault lies only in yourself. Abuse no one and nothing, for abuse turns the wise ones to fools and robs the spirit of its vision. When it comes your time to die, be not like those whose hearts are filled with fear of death, so that when their time comes they weep and pray for a little more time to live their lives over again in a different way. Sing your death song and die like a hero going home."

-Chief Tecumseh

It's the work that we do in ourselves
that's the most important.

*This is what
feeds the world.*

The journey of the heart doesn't require us to participate in any kind of religion, it doesn't ask for a college education, and we don't have to all sit in nirvana on the top of a mountain, or go anywhere for that matter. It simply requires a human being (you got that one) who wants to participate in their journey, to be present to their fullest experience of life, to know themselves from a plan that reflects their truth and their love.

Yes, doing the work of becoming you, coming to know your own heart, your spirited identity, creates a bigger energy field by far than just talking or thinking about it. Talking about it and thinking about it helps lay some groundwork, *but the power lays in the doing!*

Yup, make a *big* splash in the universe, become a willing participant in your own journey.

Our thoughts are all very real, but they're not always true. So, of course, we don't need to give our attention to every one of them, or sometimes any of them! Learn discernment, and always try to wander toward a gentler way—one that your heart knows.

JOURNEY PROMPT

Watch your mind. How many thoughts beg for your attention with only the promise of leading you into pain and distraction from your peace? Is it worth it?

"Live in each season as it passes; breathe the air and resign yourself to the influence of the earth."
-Henry David Thoreau

It's important to watch how the mind entertains its thinking.

We can catch ourselves entertaining negative thoughts that we know only bring us down. But we're in charge. We give life to the chattering in our heads that says, "I don't belong," or, "I'm not enough," and then we're the ones who mistakenly reflect that into our world. Remember, it has no truth to it. It's just a glitch; an old habit of the mind.

Pay attention to yourself. Ask life's difficult questions and listen to the answers:

Who am I at my core?

- What's really important?
- How do I live my life and be true to myself?
- How hard do I judge other people? Or myself?
- How accepting am I of my own uniqueness?
- How accepting am I of other people's differences?
- Do I know trust, forgiveness, compassion, and love?

Listen to all your answers—listen to the loud ones and the ones that hide and feel shameful. They hold a hidden influence, and the ones that hold the energy of the heart are the ones you can breathe through. It's these answers that reflect the paradigm of how you walk through your world; these are the lenses you use to see yourself with, and determine how you approach those you care about.

JOURNEY PROMPT
Give yourself the gift of *love* and *open-hearted belonging*.

Looking in the mirror, look into your own eyes, and say and these words:

> **You're enough.**
> **You belong.**
> **You're lovable.**
> **You make a difference.**

Pay attention to the discomforts and glitchy feelings around each of these statements. That's where your work begins as you journey towards the truth and love of yourself.

HUMAN THOUGHT ATTACK

Allow yourself to step back and identify that you are caught up in crappy thoughts and that you need to wait them out and allow them to shift naturally, with the understanding that clear thoughts will absolutely become available.

Just keep saying, "It's just a thought," and let it pass. Being in a "thought attack" does not define anything about your truth. It just means you're experiencing a distortion of thinking, which automatically pulls you away from your true nature of peace and separates you from your inspired wisdom. So, leave it be. Allow it to naturally flow away. Understand it is just a thought and know that as it flows past, your mind does not have to entertain it. This opens your heart and mind to fresh thought—a quality of thinking that welcomes peace and invites the expression of your true nature and your natural wisdom to move through you.

JOURNEY PROMPT

Do three things with this entry:

1. Read it to yourself when you're stuck. Read it slowly, considering each line, and allow it to help you open.

2. Find a quiet place alone and read it to yourself out loud, slowly, considering each line, and allow it to help you open.

3. Read this to someone you love when they're struggling or when the time feels right. Read it slowly, considering each line, and allow it to help them open.

EXERCISE: STUCK IN YOUR URGES

Give your body ten minutes to physiologically shift around and past your urges. Don't just immediately give in. That's not what your body really wants. Urges are there to let you know you're off balance somehow, because they're not needs, they're wants. If you recognize an urge of any kind—let's say for any kind of food or drink or addiction—make it a point to wait a bit for your wisdom to catch up with your desire.

Wait ten, fifteen, or twenty minutes (whatever works for you), and give yourself the opportunity to look at the urge in a less seductive way, making room for a more gentle and healthy choice.

The objective here, as with all conscious experience, is to connect with something inside yourself that expresses your gentleness and simultaneously maintains your strength.

Tapping Into YOUR PERSONAL PRESENCE

So, here's my story. It's about doughnuts. Mind you, I barely ever eat doughnuts nowadays, but in the old days, I used to jump right in with a big smile and an open mouth, I looked kind of like Homer Simpson! But now, when I drive past my favorite doughnut shop and that red light is on, which means those still-warm, creamy, crispy delights are ready to be ravished, I leave it alone. I know how my body feels afterwards. I know what it does to my blood sugar. I know what kind of trans fats stay in my body for months afterwards, slowly killing me after I eat them. I won't do that to myself anymore. So, I stopped eating doughnuts. But I still enjoy them! And this is how:

I've come to the conclusion that it's the joy of the experience that I love. It's the taste, texture, and the indulgence that I'm craving. It's almost like a self-love, like a self-induced happiness, but I want it without the self-induced damage. So, I play it through my mind like a movie—the act of eating my nice fresh, warm doughnut, tasting it, remembering what it feels like on the tongue, to have that first slightly crunchy bite with its warm, almost unperceivable dough bread underneath. It's so light and fluffy, it's as though you're eating a cloud. I love it! I give myself that joyful experience every time I drive by. I feel myself salivating and smiling and enjoying my doughnut, all without the need to actually partake in the doughnut doom, which, despite the joy, always leaves me feeling sick.

Remembering my doughnut experience is very satisfying, and I've come to the conclusion that it satiates a place in my brain that just wants to feel joy and nurturing. Eating these little fellas is joyfully burned into my memory, so why not use that to rekindle the best part of the experience while putting the bad parts in perspective? It works, and I never feel compelled to stop at the shop because I've already had and thoroughly enjoyed the best parts of my doughnut.

Tapping Into YOUR PERSONAL PRESENCE

Moral note to self: This probably works for more than just doughnuts.

MONKEY MIND

The concept of "Monkey Mind" is derived through the Buddhist idea that our minds can easily be distracted and become undisciplined, that they can get scattered and out of control at the drop of a pin, not unlike a tree full of monkeys. Monkeys can become easily distracted by just about everything: food, weather, sounds, and especially other monkeys. Sound familiar? Ever feel this way?

It's hard to deal with living our lives reliant on where our scattered and arbitrary thinking takes us, thinking that seems to spontaneously arise, sometimes with absolutely no reason behind it. When we react to whatever enters

Tapping Into YOUR PERSONAL PRESENCE

our head, believe our every thought, that's the monkey thinking. It takes us away, out of any sense of presence or mindfulness. There's not much in the form of quiet in this kind of thought. We need to bring a certain presence and discernment into our thinking, to pull ourselves back into a state of mind that's not so unruly and frantic, and to create a way of being in our lives that's not so vulnerable to the world around it. There's some choice involved in our journey towards not minding the monkeys in our head. It requires that we cultivate an understanding of our own mind and its tendencies to distract, perhaps for it's own sense of safety in the wild. But we're in a different world now, with a different capacity for consciousness, and we need to develop a drive within ourselves to recognize the symptoms of giving into and getting lost in a world that seems to be whirling around us, a world whipping on by with a bunch of flying monkeys paving its path. We're asked to weather and not participate in the storm, choosing instead to maintain our center and presence of simply being in the moment, whatever it brings, and rather than getting frantic monkey syndrome, just doing what needs to be done with a presence that doesn't require us to get lost in the whirling world. Pay attention to the quality of thinking that you entertain and interact with. When we let the monkeys reign, we can get stuck in some very unpleasant places as well as some distracted places that we think seem pretty nice, but, regardless, we're missing the point of being present in a full way to the life unfolding to us. We're allowing ourselves to be sidetracked by the monkeys from being fully present and fully alive to everything life is, without distracted attachment. Simply stated, in mindfulness, we cultivate a state of being and a position of centered strength that helps us to be in our lives more gracefully.

Tapping Into YOUR PERSONAL PRESENCE

When we're stuck in our arbitrary thinking, to the attached monkey mind, it seems to be anything but arbitrary. But the monkey is *very* real, and when it chimes into our lives, it thinks it owns the place, and boy does it get busy with its serious and very important business of keeping our heads in the game, crazy or not! It's hard to look at anything else until you call your monkey out on its game, until you recognize the monkey business for what it is—distraction from gracefully being in your world.

JOURNEY PROMPT

So, yes, the unkept human mind can feel like it's filled with drunken monkeys, jumping all over the place, chattering nonstop, keeping our minds in constant, uncontrolled, unsettled, and often mischievous motion.

In identifying that there's a monkey jumping around in your head, what do you do? The simple answer is to ignore it, let them settle, because they will, and without your attention and belief in your fear-based and arbitrary monkey thinking, those thoughts will naturally settle away. Understand that it's part of the human condition to get stuck in our thinking. Perhaps it's a survival technique from the past when wild animals needed to be attended to. But now, we get more out of letting our frantic thinking settle away, and in letting our thought shift into something more mindful. We find a space within where we can again be present to our lives. That's the nature of thought. It

Tapping Into YOUR PERSONAL PRESENCE

flows through, and when we don't grab on to tense and frantic thinking, new qualities of thought quite automatically unfold. Our job is to maintain our attention on the center of our own true nature, to know peace and the presence of love while being in the fullness of being alive. This helps us maintain a potential for life that replaces a distracted mind with a presence that's more aligned with gratitude for life, more aligned with the peace we're meant to experience.

Monkey Mind makes it nearly impossible to slow down and enjoy the present moment. We end up taking the arbitrary thinking bouncing through our minds so seriously, believing everything running through our heads, buying into everything those problematic monkeys tell us, and it dramatically affects our personal state of wellbeing. We need to remember, that's just not our goal here, to be stuck in our heads. *Our goal is to be awake to our life.*

It can be so pleasant to just be in life. Experiencing the essence of what's surrounding us and what's within us in this one precious moment is so preferable to being stuck in compulsive thinking about where we're going or where we've been, what's next, when we are leaving, who did this or who's going to do that. We've all heard about the moment before, ignored it, gotten sidetracked. But it's really quite simple: *be here now.*

Ram Dass, *Be Here Now:* "The cosmic humor is that if you desire to move mountains and you continue to purify yourself, ultimately, you will arrive at the place where you are able to move mountains. But in order to arrive at this position of power, you will have had to give up being he-who-wanted-to-move-mountains so that you can be he-who-put-the-mountain-there-in-the-first-place. The humor is that, finally, when you have the power to move the mountain, you are the person who placed it there—so there the mountain stays."

JOURNEY PROMPT
Right here! Right now!

Being here now requires nothing but that—being wherever you are right now. The movement comes from the fact that the current moments flow forward like a river and awareness unfolds in infinite change. All you need to do is be present to it all, and fall in love with it.

No gadgets, electronics, or writing tablets necessary. In fact, they can sabotage you. In your here and now, there's no future in front of you to contemplate, and no past to ruminate over. You just have to be. Just like it says, you just have to be—here, now.

Tapping Into YOUR PERSONAL PRESENCE

My mind can be a chatterbox, an instigator, a gossiper, often making things look worse than they are, and though all this fearful jabbering is simply a product of my contaminated thought, they're still only thoughts... and I can change them.

JOURNEY PROMPT

So often, we take all of our thinking so seriously. Everything that flows through our minds seems to get the little red stickers that say "important" or "life threateningly important." We get addicted to believing everything we think, and we end up getting stuck in qualities of thought that really don't reflect who we truly are—thinking that doesn't navigate through the heart before it hits the head.

We need to extract ourselves from the habit of believing every thought that flows through our minds. The obvious ones are easy: the sky's not falling, currently there's no locust plague or real threat of nuclear disaster, and pigs don't really fly. But the ideas that we attach to based in fear, the ones that seem to be real and may, in fact, be very real, are the culprits. Between our habitual tendencies to needlessly ruminate on life and allowing the stories of our minds to mushroom without restraint, we end up stuck in very deep ways in our anxious, life-sucking thinking. We can rationalize it, find reasons we need to hold onto our fear. We end up building ourselves a world in that fear and trying to create a sense of security that's built on extremely shaky ground—ground that doesn't really support us, but simply supports more anxious thinking.

These are the thoughts that need to be seen as "only thought." These are the ones that need to be set down, released, let go of, and seen with fresh eyes so that they can be replaced by what's in our hearts, so they can retrieve a wisdom that very naturally flows through us when we are not interfering with the process because of our crafty mind.

This life, our creation, is a wonderful journey! Search for that gentle space inside you where you can span the distance between the body, mind, and spirit. Find it and allow them all to fuse together with joy, because that's what defines you.

JOURNEY PROMPT

Whether it's in the woods while sitting on a log, or on a favorite barstool in your workshop, find a place where you can sit quietly and go inside. No matter where you go, make a point of finding that one blessed internal space that allows you to quietly be you.

Tapping Into YOUR PERSONAL PRESENCE

This is where heaven begins and hell slips away. It's your internal golden cottage, the space that welcomes you to come back to yourself, the place where you can always remember your heart. You touch a deeper part of who you are and reclaim your authentic journey from here. It is through this place that you re-enter the world rejuvenated, re-calibrated, and capable of embracing life with your precious heart.

We are all thinking beings. Even if you sit there and try not to think, inevitably, thought naturally flows through your mind.

We can't choose not to think. Thought just happens. However, you can choose what kind of thinking you want to entertain. You can wallow in your pain, or you can create far more potential for cultivating peace within yourself, and, because of that, peace in the world. But it is a choice, and it's yours.

JOURNEY PROMPT

Okay, here's your challenge!

Sit there for two minutes and try not to think…

(Two minutes later.)

Did you try not to think about trying not to think? See, I prove my point. We're made to think. Thought is like a river flowing through you. You can't stop it. You can only observe it. If something flows by that you want to observe a little closer, well, it's okay to go for a swim, because you can always find the shore again.

Tapping Into YOUR PERSONAL PRESENCE

When difficult thought arises, ask yourself:

- Am I willing to give my life for this thought?
- Am I willing to spend what precious moments I have entertaining this particular quality of thinking?

Then sit quietly for a moment and allow yourself to *shift* to a softer place as you explore your answers.

JOURNEY PROMPT

It might seem like a weird question to ask yourself: **"Am I willing to give my life up for this thought?"** But if you think about it, it's actually pretty logical. There are times when we get so embroiled in our thinking that we forget to live our lives, we get stuck in our negativity and fear, and it drains our life force. So, in essence, we're giving up our precious limited moments on this earth, in this life, that we could be appreciating and embracing. We could be connecting with one another, loving our children, involving ourselves in activities we enjoy. We could even be crying about something we're sad about. Basically, we could be doing anything other than giving our lives to thinking that just doesn't deserve our attention. So, yes, we were giving up our life to that thought, and that just doesn't need to happen.

Tapping Into YOUR PERSONAL PRESENCE

> *"Look at everything as though you were seeing it either for the first or last time."*
> *-Betty Smith*

We all get caught up in the anxious thinking that stems from our belief systems, our judgments, and the fears we attach to in this world. It's the point of this place to throw us to the ground so we can pull ourselves back up. This world functions by the rule that without challenge, there can be no change. It didn't ask us if that's okay. Apparently, it thought it knew what was in our best interest.

So, sometimes we jump into our disruptive thinking in an overzealous way, eager to be right about whatever the topic of drama is in the moment. We create paranoia and anguish for ourselves and make up stories around being a victim, and attach to scenarios about us or others not being enough in this world. We spend precious time and life energy ruminating over what we don't have, not being strong enough, pretty enough, rich enough, spiritual, healthy, funny enough… We end up living life in a world of our own delusion whose only reality seems to come from believing in our stories about what we lack. But truth be known, in the deep, open-hearted reality of life, we are perfect. We're enough. We belong here just as we are, and it's through our challenges that we change, and that's just perfect.

We can reclaim ourselves, come back to our hearts, own our true identity when we stop sacrificing our peace to all that anxious thinking that encourages us to believe that we're lacking, less than, or weak.

Truth be told, we can always own the strength we were created in; the same strength that holds the identity of our true nature, the power manifested in and through our ability to know love. And knowing that love automatically resets any of these other belief systems acquired and based in fear. Knowing that we are made in love empowers us to reset all belief systems back towards our truth. And our truth is that we were made of and made through love—our truest nature. That's where our thinking belongs.

Memories often come forward, like a recorded loop of thought, and the only thing that gives them importance and life in our head is our choice to entertain them. At their best, we get to re-experience moments of love and joy, but when old memories don't work well for us, we might find ourselves stuck thinking about exactly the same event, behavior, or personal story over and over and over again until that memory owns our life and we're just totally sucked into it, no matter what its story happens to be.

Remember: All our memories, good, bad or neutral, are just looking for acknowledgment and healing, and we need to be able to put them preciously away, retrieving them and giving them life only when we choose. From here, we can approach them with good intention, fresh thought and wisdom, addressing them in new and better ways. It's a gift to that memory as well as to ourselves.

Tapping Into YOUR PERSONAL PRESENCE

JOURNEY PROMPT

Have you ever gotten caught up in an old memory about a friend or a situation that just never really felt like it worked out well, or perhaps the end was horrible? I think, at some point, everybody has, and we tend to churn that around in our minds, sometimes struggling through it and unable to let it go. That's a memory that we really need to give a little self-analysis to, because those are the kind of memories that are pretty unproductive when it comes to being in your life. They're inherently disruptive to living in this moment because they keep you in that moment.

Another scenario, that, at face, value may not seem so disruptive, is attaching to the good old days or good times. Sometimes, we want to hold onto those memories as though they're gold. But the good can be just as disruptive as the bad, because we can get lost in it, trying to hold onto it so hard that we give it a twist that keeps us yearning for those times, and we lose touch with the preciousness of where we're living now.

The point is that attaching habitually to any memories, no matter what they are, at the expense of living your life, doesn't do anybody any good. It creates a lot of unproductive tension in our thinking and can disrupt being present to our days. So, your job is to extract yourself from its compulsive story, learn whatever lessons are there to be learned, and, in a full way, step back into your life now.

Tapping Into YOUR PERSONAL PRESENCE

HEART-CENTERED BREATH EXERCISE

Find a quiet, comfortable space to be present in. Position yourself so you're either sitting in an upright position on a chair or pillow, or laying down comfortably so your body can relax into its breath. Place your right hand on your heart, your left hand on your belly, and take some comfortable breaths a little deeper and a little slower than normal. Pay attention to the movement of your hands. Your belly hand should move up and down (or for sitting, in and out) with each breath. The heart hand doesn't move much, but it does feel the energetic essence and perhaps even the beat of the heart. Spend some time in this position and very simply allow your breathing to feel as though it's opening into the heart, allowing your heart to expand with each inhale and rest with each exhale. Use your intention to maintain this position while paying attention to each breath and its movement through you.

This exercise can be as short or last as long as you would like. The objective is simple: finding some peace through the heart breath. That peace probably sprouted a little just thinking about doing the exercise. Embrace it. The heart is eager.

In truth, we already know a better way when it comes to most things in life. Deep down in our hearts, we already have the answers. It's usually just a matter of internally shutting up long enough to listen for the subtle whisper of your wisdom.

www.ingramcontent.com/pod-product-compliance
Lightning Source LLC
Chambersburg PA
CBHW021432070526
44577CB00001B/177